What people are saying...

It is a challenge to convey theological truth and faithful practice in fiction. Rev. Bramwell does so with theological deftness, pastoral winsomeness, and confessional faithfulness with regard to the challenging topic of closed Communion. Engaging, humorous, and authentic, *Come in, We Are Closed* is the helpful tool laypeople and pastors have been praying for to reach those used to open Communion. This book creatively and conversationally expands the limited number of Bible texts used to explain this faithful biblical practice within a fuller Lutheran confession of a Christian worldview and additional teaching on many other aspects of the Sacrament of the Altar. *Come in, We Are Closed* deals with Jesus' own words and how many react to them with unbelief instead of faith.

Paul J. Cain, Pastor, Immanuel Lutheran Church, Sheridan, WY; board member, Consortium for Classical Lutheran Education; author, *5 Things You Can Do to Make Your Congregation a Caring Church.*

Closed Communion is usually pictured as uninviting and lacking in grace. Through a series of cafe conversations, Pastor Bramwell portrays another picture. Using imagery from the Scriptures and early Church, the author invites readers to think about closed Communion in light of Christ's gift and our need.

John Pless, Assistant Professor of Pastoral Ministry and Missions, Concordia Theological Seminary, Fort Wayne, IN; co-editor of *Closed Communion?*

There is hardly a more sensitive issue with which pastors have to deal with than closed Communion. This is not something new, but has been exasperated by the individualism that everyone can choose what he or she wants to believe and what kind of God one wants. Pastors are trained theologically to handle closed Communion. Tyrel Bramwell fills the gap in providing real life situations that reflect how members of our churches and others see the issue. He provides enough stories so that every pastor will see a dilemma he has already faced and will most likely face. Rather than leaving the reader hanging on what the outcome should be, he provides solutions. A great strength of *Come in, We Are Closed* is its readability. The title speaks volumes. In the face of an aging and thus declining membership, our congregations and pastors are working to extend the church's boundaries. Closed Communion isn't an obstacle to church growth but an opportunity. After reading *Come in, We Are Closed*, you will see why Pastor Bramwell is among the up and coming authors in the Lutheran church.

David P. Scaer, Professor and chairman of Systematic Theology and New Testament, Concordia Theological Seminary, Fort Wayne, IN; co-author of *Understanding Four Views on the Lord's Supper.*

Pastor Bramwell carefully, yet engagingly, takes the reader through the often difficult discussion of what closed Communion is, and why it is the faithful and loving practice of the Church. Winsome characters while away the night as biblical truth seasons their conversation in a way that speaks faithfully, yet is never overbearing or forced. Most books stay put on a pastor's shelf; not this one. It will be much-loaned and highly-thumbed in years to come.

Duane Bamsch, Pastor, Zion Lutheran Church, Terra Bella, CA; Vice-President of *Higher Things.*

According to the classical education tradition, the best way to find genuine understanding is through dialectic; that is, dialogue, in which two people simply have a conversation to arrive at truth. The dialogues of Socrates took philosophy about as far as it could go. St. Anselm wrote a dialogue to explore the doctrine of Christ's Atonement. And Luther's Catechism sets up a dialogue designed to teach the Christian faith and to answer the question, "What does this mean?" Now Tyrel Bramwell has written a dialogue about the much misunderstood doctrine of Closed Communion. And in approaching the issues from unique angles, he illuminates not only this controversial practice, but Holy Communion in general, as well as the Christian faith that it embodies.

Gene Edward Veith, author of *Spirituality of the Cross.*

For some, fiction as a tool of theology is debatable. But not here. In the midst of an evening of driving snow, at the corner of one street and another, a smoky café becomes a classroom. A burley, pipe-smoking gent becomes a professor. A conversation becomes an enlightening moment for rich catechesis. And all along the way, as the winter storm keeps a steady cadence against the establishment's frame, the reader is kept warmly inside and led into a deeper understanding of what many in our radically individualized society would consider offensive: closed Communion. A finely crafted narrative, Bramwell sets out to sort through the sorest contours of the subject while at the same time giving a clear witness to the Word of God and the genuine love that is inherent to the practice.

Christopher Thoma, Pastor, Our Savior Evangelical Lutheran Church, Hartland, MI; author of *The Angels' Portion* series.

Explaining closed Communion can be a difficult task. Tyrel Bramwell offers a much needed solution with *Come in, We Are Closed*. This slim but enlightening work of fiction makes a valuable contribution to the Church. I gained new insights on why closed Communion is simply the way Communion should be done in the Church, as instructed by Holy Scripture. Closed Communion can be a hard phrase, but in reality, its practice is caring and faithful, as made clear by Bramwell's warm, instructive tale.

Ray Keating, Author of the Pastor Stephen Grant novels and short stories.

Come in, We Are Closed

TYREL BRAMWELL

ISBN-13: 978-1717081858
ISBN-10: 1717081851

To Pastor Dan Holthus,
who answered my questions

Table of Contents

Foreword

AMERICAN Christianity has developed what can be called, "my-right-to" syndrome. We have come to believe that all gifts and freedoms are intrinsically given and/or by divine right afforded to us based on the fact that we merely exist.

So, what, dear Christian, do you deserve? We deserve death and hell. Yet, Christ in His mercy has given us grace in His most Holy Sacrament. It isn't a "right." It is much more than that.

What we receive from the Holy Altar of God is the pure and unadulterated forgiveness of sins. We are given Christ's own self that He would tabernacle with us and we would be His branches. We are not afforded the right, but we are lovingly invited to join the wedding feast of the Lamb in His kingdom even though we are not yet in heaven.

What we have in receiving the body and the blood of Jesus Christ is a gift that 1 Corinthians tells us we are to receive in the true confession of what is on the altar. Otherwise, we should be very afraid to receive it.

With that said, you will find in this book the gentlest way of explaining closed Communion. You will read that not all are welcomed to the table of the Lord. Those who are, partake in the life-giving Sacrament that gives us the forgiveness of sins and therefore our own salvation through Jesus Christ our Lord.

The explanation in this book is kind, loving, and completely in agreement with Scripture. Remember as you read this book that closed Communion is not some weird form of exclusivity, but the Biblical duty of called and ordained pastors. Is there a greater blessing than a faithful pastor who administers the Sacraments according to the Holy Bible?

My friend, Rev. Bramwell, practices this faithfully and we would be remiss if we tossed out this book as mere opinion. In short, read this book and compare it with Scripture. I think you will find a friendly understanding of closed Communion. If not, I recommend reading it again.

Rev. Gaven M. Mize
Augustana Evangelical Lutheran Church
Hickory, North Carolina
Day of Pentecost, 2018

The Wedding Rehearsal

WIND whipped snow pellets against my face as I crunched toward the café doors. I unwrapped my scarf and looked up at the hostess.

"Smoking or non?" she asked.

Normally I would have requested non, but as I surveyed the café's smoking section it looked warm and inviting. The air was thicker than the non-smoking section, like a blanket I could use to warm myself.

"Smoking, please."

She led me to a booth, took my order for coffee, and disappeared into the kitchen. As I sat down I noticed a man looking at me. He was seated in the booth next to mine. I greeted him with a nod. He returned it. He had gentle eyes buried in weather-worn sockets. The rest of his face was covered by a shaggy grey beard that extended from high on his cheeks to just past his collar bone, hair shooting every which way. The hair on his head was long and matted down from where a hat would ride. It shone under the café lights. He wore a striped, multicolored sweater that had seen better days. It was peppered with holes and strands of yarn that coiled away from the weave as if not to be outdone by the man's beard. The smell of tobacco preceded him. I spotted its source. A pipe.

"Cold night," I said.

He nodded, looked out the window, and hummed his agreement. The waitress returned with my coffee. She left a carafe. As I sipped the cup of liquid warmth, the man said, "The temperature plummets when the sun goes down."

"Isn't that the truth," I responded. "It's cold enough during the day. When it's dark, it's downright unbearable."

"A guy is glad to be in out of it, that's for sure," the man said. Something about the way he said it made me think he appreciated being at the café more than most.

I blew steam off my coffee.

"Did you brave the weather just for that cup of joe?" he said.

"Not exactly," I replied. "I was already out. Thought I'd pop in for a cup, or a carafe as it were." I picked up the pitcher and grinned.

"Why not?" the man said.

Our conversation continued, and before I knew it he invited me to his booth and made our conversation more than passing pleasantries.

I didn't catch his full name, but he said his friends called him Shep, a nickname he was fond of because it was derived from his days as a pastor. This bit of information shaped our entire conversation. I don't know if we would have had much to talk about otherwise.

"I'm glad I bumped into you, Shep," I said. "Given that you were a pastor, do you mind if I ask you a church question?"

"Not at all."

"All right, so, what do you know about churches that don't let some people take Communion?"

Shep puffed on his pipe while I spoke. As my question took shape, a welcoming smile emerged around the bit. He lowered his pipe and the smoke that was wallowing up between us dissipated. "Did you have a bad experience with closed Communion?"

"Is that what it's called?"

"It is."

"I wouldn't call it *bad*. It's just not very inviting, you know? I assume churches want people to feel welcome, and, well, that's not very welcoming."

"You're right. Churches do want people to feel welcome. Believe it or not, closed Communion isn't meant to keep folks from participating in the Lord's Supper, but to get them to His Table where they can receive God's gifts."

There must have been a strange look on my face, because Shep stopped speaking, leaned over, and from a dingy mound of clothing next to him he pulled out an old tattered book. His Bible.

I drank my coffee.

When I put my mug back on the table Shep continued, "Are you familiar with Jesus' parable of the wedding feast?" He fingered the Bible's thin pages. "It's here at the beginning of Matthew 22." He traced the words with a boney index finger. There was something strange about the text.

"What language is that?" I said.

Shep looked up. "Oh, this is my Greek New Testament." He could see I wanted more information. "Vocational hazard, I'm afraid. Reading Scripture in the original languages is helpful." He went back to the text.

I liked that.

A moment passed and he looked up again. "So, are you familiar with the parable?" he asked.

"Oh, sorry. No," I said. "Not very. Maybe a little. What's it say?"

Shep began to read, "The Kingdom of Heaven is like a certain king, who made a marriage feast for his son." He pulled his head from the page and said, "Do you know who we're talking about here?"

I did. "Jesus, the Son of God."

"Good," Shep said, and then continued from his Bible. "The king sent out his servants to call those who were invited to the marriage feast, but they would not come." He looked up again. "You mentioned that closed Communion wasn't very inviting. It didn't make you feel very welcome. You were on to something." He sucked life into the bowl of his pipe and then exhaled smoke from his mouth.

"And what's that?" I asked while I refilled my cup.

"You need to be invited to take Communion. The Lord's Table isn't like this café, where you can come as you are and eat what you want when you want because you want it. It's a foretaste of the heavenly wedding feast. There's a little more to it than an open buffet. The king—God—invited people to attend His Son's wedding, but because they weren't worthy they wouldn't come. So, He sent out more servants who told them that the king had prepared the wedding feast. Their job was to deliver the wedding invitations." Shep looked back at his Bible. "Come to the marriage feast!" and then he looked at me. "It was a direct invitation to eat at the king's banquet. Have you ever been invited to a wedding?"

I nodded.

"Did you go?"

I nodded again.

"Did you just show up on that day or did you RSVP?"

"I RSVPed."

"Good. Well, the original guests invited to the prince's wedding made light of their invitation. It would be like they didn't bother to RSVP, like they ripped up the invitation and in some cases, even killed the postman who delivered it."

"Okay," I said. "Jesus' parable says heaven comes by way of an invitation; what does that have to do with Communion?"

Shep smiled. I could tell he liked to smile. It looked good on his face. Natural. "Communion is a dress rehearsal for that wedding. It's where we practice for the big day. In fact, it's heaven on earth, a foretaste of the marriage feast of the Lamb." He took another drag from his pipe and then said, "This isn't the only place in Scripture where heaven is talked about in terms of a wedding feast."

"Oh, yeah?"

"Revelation 19 says," he plopped over a bunch of pages, swiped a few more, and found his spot, "'Let us rejoice and be exceedingly glad, and let us give the glory to Him'—*Christ*—'For the marriage of the Lamb has come, and His wife'—*the Church*—'has made herself ready. It was given to her that she would array herself in bright, pure, fine linen: for the fine linen is the righteous acts of the saints.'" He paused and tapped his fingertip on the page. "'Blessed are those who are invited to the marriage supper of the Lamb.'" He looked up as he spoke the last sentence, "These are true words of God."

"Okay, but I have been invited. I'm a Christian."

Shep smiled. "I'm glad to hear that."

"That's why I don't understand why a church would say I can't take Communion. Closed Communion acts like I haven't been invited to the wedding."

I took a sip and looked over the edge of my cup for Shep's response. He swallowed his coffee and replied, "Does it act like you haven't been invited, or like you haven't RSVPed?"

"What do you mean?"

"You were invited to the wedding. You'd be hard pressed to find a Christian church that would deny that. But did you RSVP?"

"That's why I was in church," I said.

"No, no. That's not RSVPing. That's showing up to the wedding rehearsal unannounced."

"Wait, you're saying that if I want to take Communion, I have to let them know ahead of time?"

"That would be polite," he said, and then inhaled his tobacco. As he released it from his lungs he said, "When you RSVPed to the wedding you attended, was there a meal at the reception?"

"Yeah."

"And when you RSVPed, that helped the host know to expect you, right?"

"Sure," I said inquisitively.

"You made it known that you had received an invitation, and unlike the rude guests in the parable, you didn't take it lightly, but took note of it and responded to it. You declared that you would attend."

"Right. The would-be guests in the parable couldn't be bothered to come to the wedding. But I went to church because I was invited," I said.

"Because you didn't take the invitation lightly."

"Exactly."

"No doubt, you reacted to the invitation. Consider the rest of Jesus' parable. The king doesn't take too kindly to being snubbed. He sends his army to destroy those who rejected his invitation, and then he expands who he invites to anyone and everyone who could be found."

Shep dropped his head to the page. "The text says that the king said to his servants, 'The wedding is ready, but those who were invited weren't worthy. Go therefore to the intersections of the highways, and as many as you may find, invite to the marriage feast.'"

Shep put the book down and sipped some coffee before saying, "The invitation went out to everyone. The king was very inviting, very welcoming. Like you expected the church you attended to be, right?"

"Yeah. Everyone is welcome. That's inviting. That's how God is," I said.

"Yes, He is. He welcomes everyone. And if I was a betting man, I'd say the closed Communion church you attended aims to welcome everyone, too. But there is more to it. Wedding guests don't get to come as they are."

I made a sound that indicated I didn't understand.

"When you attended the wedding, weren't the guests expected to behave a certain way when they arrived? For instance, you weren't allowed to sit at the head table, were you?"

"Of course not, that's reserved for the wedding party."

"So, if you don't feel entitled to that table, why would you feel entitled to sit, or kneel rather, at the Lord's Table?"

Again, I think my expression betrayed me, because Shep continued with further explanation. "Keep listening. 'Those servants went out into the highways, and gathered together as many as they found, both bad and good.'"

For emphasis Shep repeated that both *bad* and *good* are welcome at the heavenly wedding feast, and then continued reading, "'The wedding was filled with guests. But when the king came in to see the guests, he saw there a man who didn't have on wedding clothing, and he said to him, 'Friend, how did you come in here not wearing wedding clothing?' He was speechless. Then the king said to the servants, 'Bind him hand and foot, take him away, and throw him into the outer darkness; there is where the weeping and grinding of teeth will be.' For many are called, but few chosen.'"

Shep looked out the window.

"It's easy to understand closed Communion when you think of it in terms of this parable," he said, his attention captivated by the snowy night. "The king not only invited everyone he could find, but he gave them the clothes they needed to attend. He's welcoming, but He doesn't tolerate wedding crashers." He looked at me. "Did you wear nice clothes to the wedding you attended?"

I nodded.

"Good. Dressing for the occasion is a dying art these days." We both took a drink and he continued talking. "God is inviting, welcoming, so much so that not only does He invite everyone to His Son's wedding feast, He also provides them with what they need to attend. Everyone who RSVPed wore the king's clothing, Christ's robe of righteousness."

Shep let his words settle for a moment and then continued. "Closed Communion, the entire worship service really, is a rehearsal for the marriage feast of the Lamb to come, for heaven. The invitations have been sent out. John 3:16, right?"

"Sure," I said, "'For God so loved the world, that He gave His one and only Son, that whoever believes in Him should not perish, but have eternal life.'"

"Right, when the pastor stands in the pulpit and preaches God's Gospel message, he's sending out the invitation for everyone to attend Jesus' wedding. He tells his hearers that God has invited them to His Son's wedding, and that because they're sinners He has even provided the clothing necessary for the black tie affair. That's for everybody. He's one of the king's servants inviting the bad and the good alike, anybody and everybody, to come to the wedding and, therefore, to participate in the dress rehearsal.

"When you were visiting the church, you were there as one who had heard the invitation. You didn't reject it. But how was the pastor or the ushers or anybody there supposed to know you were there for the rehearsal? As far as they knew you could've just been some passerby who noticed the activity and peeked in to see what was going on."

I topped off my coffee cup as Shep spoke. His cup was low, too. I gestured toward the carafe and then toward his cup. "Yes, please," he said, and we watched the brown drink rise. "Thank you."

"So, how do I RSVP?" I asked.

"The man in the parable wanted to attend the wedding feast without putting on the king's wedding clothing. RSVPing is putting on God's wedding garment."

"You said that was Christ's robe of righteousness?"

"That's right," Shep said. "There's an account in the book of Acts. It's wonderful to think on." Shep fanned his Bible's pages to a sermon preached by Peter. "Peter told his hearers about Jesus. He invited them to heaven, to the wedding feast. After he extended God's invitation they responded by wanting to know how to be saved. You could say they wanted to know what to do with the invitation. Peter said,

'Repent, and be baptized, every one of you, in the name of Jesus Christ for the forgiveness of sins, and you will receive the gift of the Holy Spirit. For the promise is to you, and to your children, and to all who are far off, even as many as the Lord our God will call to himself.'"

Shep pressed his shoulders into the back of the booth and again his smile surfaced. He held up his Bible. The pages drooped over his hands. He tapped the bit of his pipe against the page and tipped the book toward him so he could read it. "'So those who received his word were baptized. There were added that day about three thousand souls.'"

I chewed on what I had heard for a minute. The waitress returned.

"You two doing okay?" she said.

"Yes, ma'am," Shep said.

"Me, too," I added.

Shep looked at me, smiled, and said, "In Galatians 3, Paul said, 'For you are all children of God, through faith in Christ Jesus. For as many of you as were baptized into Christ have *put on* Christ.'"

I considered Paul's words and connected it to Jesus' parable of the wedding feast. "The guy who was thrown out, it was because he didn't have on the wedding clothing?"

"Exactly. Even though he was on the guest list, he thought he'd crash the wedding. Communion is the rehearsal for the marriage feast of the Lamb. Closed Communion is the Church being honest at the rehearsal about what's to come. If you think about it, it's actually the only welcoming way to do Communion."

"What do you mean?" I said.

"Think about the churches that don't practice closed Communion, the ones who have an open Communion policy, they're not exactly practicing for Heaven the way Heaven is, now are they? Jesus said Heaven is like a wedding feast where a guy gets thrown into the outer darkness," Shep thumbed toward the window, "because he thought he could be there on his own terms. Open Communion encourages a false view of God and heaven; it welcomes people to practice something that isn't preparing them for the event to come. A church that practices closed Communion is a church that invites anybody and everybody to Heaven and then prepares them to be welcomed at the Lord's marriage feast when He finally returns."

Shep looked out the window. He focused in on the snow blowing past the parking lot lights. Beyond the white glow there was nothing but black. "Can I tell you something?" Shep said.

"Of course."

"I think it's good that you were a little put off by closed Communion."

I smirked. "Why is that?"

"Because that's what rehearsals are for. That's the time to ask the questions, that's the time to make the mistakes and ease the nerves." Shep tipped over his pipe and rapped it on the edge of the ash tray. "It's better to learn the truth now than to be unprepared for what's to come."

I nodded in agreement.

Shut Out

SHEP had invited me to his table. When I arrived at the café, I didn't expect to have a conversation with a stranger. I thought I'd sit for a while in my own little world, in a warm booth, out of the cold.

"I appreciate you entertaining my questions, Shep."

"It's been my pleasure," he said.

"I hope I'm not taking up too much of your time."

"Not at all."

"If I'm holding you up, just say the word."

"I appreciate that," Shep said, "but on a night like tonight this is about it for me." He nodded toward the window. "It's good to be in where it's warm."

"That's for sure," I said. "No one wants to be out in that."

We sat in silence for a minute. I fiddled with my half empty coffee cup while Shep tended to his pipe. Finally, I spoke. "It never would have occurred to me to think of Communion as a dress rehearsal for heaven."

"But that's exactly what it is, a foretaste of the feast to come," Shep said.

I nodded and looked around the room in thought. There was a door that separated the café lobby from the kitchen. I couldn't see much of the kitchen, just the waitresses going in and coming out. "Like ordering an appetizer before your meal?" I said.

Shep was lighting his pipe with a match. I could hear the sizzle of the flame on the tobacco. He chomped down on the bit, looked at me past the burning bowl, and said, "Something like that." He crossed his eyes as he focused on the glowing embers inches from his face. A second later a sweet smell filled my nose.

While still somewhat preoccupied with his tobacco, Shep reiterated that a dress rehearsal is preparation for the wedding just like Communion is preparation for the coming of the Lord. He then drew my attention back to his Bible and said, "When we were talking about the parable of the wedding feast, if we would have kept reading, we would have heard another parable in chapter twenty-five, the one about the ten virgins."

"I'm familiar," I said. "Some are wise and some are foolish, right?"

"That's right, and just like the parable of the wedding feast, it shows us that closed Communion is the good and right way to prepare believers for heaven."

"How so?" I asked.

"First of all, it's about the coming of the Bridegroom."

"Jesus."

"Right. Jesus. In the parable of the wedding feast He's the prince getting married. John calls it the marriage of the Lamb in Revelation 19." Shep inhaled and spoke smoky words. "Well, in this parable Jesus says that, 'the Kingdom of Heaven will be like ten virgins, who took their lamps, and went out to meet the bridegroom.' Like you said, five of them were foolish, and five were wise. Those who were foolish, when they took their lamps, took no oil with them, but the wise took oil in their vessels with their lamps." He paused. "How are we on coffee?"

I picked up the carafe and shook it. It sloshed.

"We could use a refill."

"Let's see if we can flag down the waitress," Shep said, and then extended his hand like a flag hoisted up a pole.

The waitress caught his movement and I held up the empty evidence that we were in need of her service. When she arrived she quipped, "Depleted the reserves, I see," and then assured us that she would be back in a minute with some more.

Shep continued, "Now while the bridegroom delayed, the virgins slumbered and slept. But at midnight there was a cry, 'Behold! The bridegroom is coming! Come out to meet him!' Then all those virgins arose, and trimmed their lamps. The foolish said to the wise, 'Give us some of your oil, for our lamps are going out.' But the wise answered, saying, 'What if there isn't enough for us and you? You go rather to those who sell, and buy for yourselves.' While they went away to buy, the bridegroom came, and those who were ready went in with him to the marriage feast, and the door was shut. Afterward the other virgins also came, saying, 'Lord, Lord, open to us.' But he answered, 'Most certainly I tell you, I don't know you.' Watch therefore, for you don't know the day nor the hour in which the Son of Man is coming." Shep puffed on his pipe and waited for me to say something.

"I get the message about being prepared, but I'm a little hazy on how the preparation relates to Communion." I lifted my cup to my lips to take a drink but stopped short and asked,

"Because it has to do with the coming of the Bridegroom, heaven as a marriage feast?"

Shep smiled at my question, which was really more of an assessment.

"That's the setting, isn't it?" he said. "The message, like you said, is about being prepared to go into the marriage feast when the Bridegroom comes. This parable reveals that there will be people who are shut out of the banquet hall—heaven—because they weren't prepared."

"Because they didn't practice for His coming properly," I said.

I could see why Shep's eyes were wrinkled. He was old, but I suspected that it had more to do with his smile. His crow's feet had crow's feet. I imagined it was from a lifetime of smiling just like he was now.

"Not practicing properly, or at all." he said. "This parable reveals something about the relationship between Baptism and Communion."

I shifted in my seat.

"All of the virgins have a lamp with which they go out to meet the bridegroom. They're all waiting for the wedding day. They've heard the Gospel, they believe. We can understand the parable's language to be saying that there was a group of believers, waiting for the Lord's return. The virgins are baptized, Bible-believing Christians, right?"

"Okay," I said.

"In other words, they're the Church." Shep held up his coffee cup and said, "They all have been given a lamp by which to see." He took a drink. "As we heard—and as we know ourselves given that it's been about 2000 years since Jesus ascended into heaven—the Bridegroom has been delayed." He deposited his cup on the table, picked up his pipe, and pointed it at me. "Some of the virgins were prepared for this delay. They made sure they had plenty of oil for their Baptism lamps."

"And some didn't," I added.

"Nothing worse than needing a flashlight only to find out that the batteries are dead," Shep said. "It's like having a pocket knife too dull to cut anything." He bit his lower lip in contemplation, as if he was remembering a time his knife or flashlight had failed him.

The waitress returned with another carafe. "Here you are." She poured its contents into my mug first and then Shep's. "Let me know when you need some more. I have a new pot on."

As if on cue we both said, "Thank you."

"You bet. On a night like this, we gotta keep it flowing," she said and then moved to a booth behind Shep. She checked in on the occupants, and was just as polite to them as she had been to us.

Shep looked at his Greek New Testament. When he was assured that the welcomed interruption was over, he said, "The foolish virgins didn't have oil for their Baptism lamps. They had lamps, but over time, while the Bridegroom was delayed, the oil inside—their faith—evaporated. At the end of the parable Jesus says, 'Watch therefore, for you don't know the day nor the hour in which the Son of Man is coming.' In other words, be vigilant, be prepared."

"So, you're saying that the relationship between Baptism and Communion is like a lamp and its oil?" I asked.

"Yes. Christians need to have their faith fed. When you're given faith, if it isn't cared for, it'll weaken and run out," Shep said.

"And you feed your faith at Communion?" I said.

"That's where Jesus gives you His body to eat," he said. "The wise virgins told the fools to go to the sellers to get oil for their lamps. They're told to go to church, go where God's pastors distribute the goods we need to live." Shep put his pipe in his mouth and held up a skeletal finger. "Hold on," he mumbled as he rummaged through his coat piled beside him. He sat up with another book in his hand.

"What's that?" I asked.

"The Old Testament." He looked a little embarrassed, and with the pipe in his mouth he murmured, "Hebrew."

"You read Greek *and* Hebrew?"

"You'll have to excuse me. My Hebrew isn't as good as my Greek."

I leaned back and grinned, "Well, I guess I can let that slide."

Shep smiled and said, "But, never you fear. I'm still proficient enough, plus I have all these notes from over the years." He allowed me to inspect his Old Testament. It was full of notes. After I gave it a glance he flipped the pages and got us back on track. "See, the 'sellers' are at church. They're the clergymen who celebrate Communion. Listen to Isaiah's language here in chapter 55, how he talks about water and wine, the same elements used in Baptism and Communion. He says, 'Come, everyone who thirsts, to the waters! Come, he who has no money, buy, and eat! Yes, come, buy wine and milk without money and without price. Why do you spend money for that which is not bread, and your labor for that which doesn't satisfy? Listen diligently to me, and eat that which is good, and let your soul delight itself in richness. Turn your ear, and come to me. Hear, and your soul will live.'" Shep looked up. "Like you and I came to this café to get something warm to drink, Christians have a place to go and buy what they need to have eternal life, only the buying is done without money because God is gracious and giving. Just as He freely gave the wedding garment in Matthew 22, He freely gives the lamps and oil—faith—so that there is no reason the virgins should be shut out of the wedding hall."

I said, "The foolish virgins weren't prepared."

"Right."

"They could've been, if only they would've continued going to church?"

"Yes. They were given faith, their Baptism lamps, but they weren't watchful. They didn't go to church where they would've heard God's Word preached, where they would've received Communion—their oil—and been assured of the forgiveness of their sins."

I took a sip of coffee.

He continued, "This is one very important reason why Christians need to be in church on a regular basis. They need to be watchful, they need to have their lamp oil filled. Communion, which is the center of the Church's worship, is where we're made wise, it's where we're prepared for the coming of the Bridegroom, where we learn what His arrival will be like, what the marriage feast will be like, and how we're made participants in all of the eternal celebration." Shep looked out the window again. "Honestly, look at it out there."

I looked. It was dark. I could hear the wind whistling. A car pulled into the parking lot. The snow blew across the beam of the headlights. I wasn't ready to venture back out in that cold.

Shep's voice pulled my gaze from the iced over concrete and cars and back into the restaurant. "Who wants to be shut out in the dark?"

I took his question to be rhetorical, but thought to myself, "not me." My mind went in another direction. There was something I hadn't thought much about, something the two parables Shep showed me called to my attention. There will be a time when God will permanently bring people into heaven—the marriage feast of the Lamb—or shut them out of it. Shep was making an argument that said the closed Communion practice refused to let people forget that, and for the best possible reason: to keep people from being shut out. I wasn't used to closed Communion. I didn't understand it, but now I wanted to. What I was used to, what I supposed would be called open Communion, didn't seem to be consistent with the coming of the Bridegroom. At least it didn't proclaim the reality that God would one day close a door and say to those on the outside, "I don't know you."

Shep could see that I was deep in thought. Eventually he interrupted my contemplation. "The reason churches practice closed Communion is because they don't want anyone to be shut out on the Last Day. God doesn't either." Shep flopped his pages over and said, "Consider all of this in light of what happened in the garden of Eden." He skimmed over the words and said, "After Adam and Eve ate of the tree of the knowledge of good and evil, before they could eat of the tree of life and live forever knowing evil, 'the Lord God sent them out of the garden of Eden.' You could say God was the first one to practice closed Communion."

"Wait," I said. "You're comparing Adam and Eve eating from the tree of the knowledge of good and evil with us eating the Lord's Supper?"

"There's a comparison to be made, but no," Shep said. "I'm comparing the Lord's Supper to eating from the tree of life, which they weren't allowed to do while they knew evil. God implemented a closed Communion policy and shut them out of the garden for their own good, so they wouldn't live forever in their foolish sin." Shep read some more, "God drove out the man; and he placed cherubim at the east of the garden of Eden, and a flaming sword which turned every way, to guard the way to the tree of life."

"So what changed?" I asked.

Shep looked at me inquisitively.

"Something had to change before people could receive Communion. Why would God bar Adam and Eve, but not everyone who takes Communion?"

"Great question," Shep said. "Something did change. Jesus died on the cross. He undid the evil Adam unleashed on mankind. The cross of

Christ is the tree of life, and all who know good and repent of evil now eat of its fruit—the body and blood of Jesus—so that they'll live forever in Communion with God. You see, sometimes, God prohibits people from eating as a benefit to them. That's why the Church practices closed Communion. It's not to be rude, but for the well-being of sinners, so that when they eat of the tree of life they'll live forever knowing only good."

I didn't say anything. I didn't know what to say. Shep sat patiently with his two testaments in front of him. It was like he knew I needed some time to mull over what Scripture said. I did.

A Little History

SHEP had well thought out answers to my questions, but each one stirred a new thought in my mind.

"Okay, Shep. So, why isn't closed Communion more common?"

Shep looked at me, smacked his lips, and said, "Oh, but it's very common."

"I've been to more than a few different churches. The one that said I couldn't commune was the first I encountered to say such a thing."

Shep just smiled.

"What?" I said.

"My friend, perhaps you've been going to the wrong churches."

I didn't respond.

Shep said, "Let me give you a little history."

"Okay."

"What we call closed Communion is the Church's historic practice." He drummed his fingers on the Old Testament. "It goes all the way back to Eden." With his pipe in his mouth he drummed the fingers of his other hand on the New Testament. "On the night Jesus instituted the Lord's Supper, we see that it was a private event our Lord hosted in the upper room for His closest followers, the twelve disciples. Today, many churches don't revere the Sacrament as they should, but not so with the early Church. In the first centuries of Christianity, if you were not a member of the Church, you could come to hear the Bible readings, sing hymns, listen to the sermon, and pray, but not even those who were being instructed in the Faith could attend the Service of the Sacrament."

I interjected. "Really? They couldn't even attend the service?"

"That's right. Anyone with an unconfirmed faith had to leave. The doors of the church would be closed and even guarded," Shep said.

"Guarded?"

"Not by cherubim with flaming swords, but by the deacons. Like God, they took it seriously."

"I guess so," I said with a stunned look on my face.

"We get the term closed Communion from the closed doors."

"Interesting."

"It was a pretty powerful dress rehearsal, wouldn't you say?"

I swallowed my drink. "Oh, yeah."

"If you wanted to take Communion, the clergy needed to know you."

"Like Jesus said to the foolish virgins," I said.

Shep's look invited me to elaborate.

"When the foolish virgins were shut out of the wedding feast, the Bridegroom said He didn't know them," I said.

"That's good. Yes. Like the Bridegroom, the pastors who stand in His stead need to know the Christian who wishes to Commune." Shep shifted his pipe from one hand to the other. "Of course, the local pastors knew who was under their care." He paused, inspected his pipe, and returned it to its original hand. "Or, if you'd rather, who had lamps and which lamps needed oil." He smiled.

I offered a grin in return. "What if you were traveling?" I said. "Could Christians take Communion when they visited other churches?"

"Yes, visitors would declare which church they belonged to. If it was an orthodox church, and they were in good standing, of course they could receive Communion."

I interrupted. "In good standing?"

"Sometimes people don't want to repent of their sins. When that happens, pastors are obligated to shepherd them—that's the job—and sometimes it means they need to withhold the Sacrament from them. The Lord's Supper is a meal for the repentant only. Communicant members in good standing are those who have been taught the Faith and repent of their sins. When those folks knew they would be traveling they could acquire a letter from their pastor to present to the church they would be visiting. If a person came from a church that taught something other than what Scripture taught, they weren't allowed to Commune. Only orthodox Christians commune at orthodox churches."

"So what defines an orthodox church?" I asked.

"That's the right question," Shep said. "Are you familiar with the word, orthodox?"

I nodded. "But, more so from *unorthodox*. Like to describe people who have an unusual way of doing things, an *unorthodox* style."

"Right. Well, the word comes from the Greek. *Ortho* means 'straight,' or 'proper.'" He took a sip. "Did you ever have braces on your teeth?"

I nodded again.

"It was the *ortho*dontist who put them on. He makes crooked teeth straight."

I smiled at the revelation. Shep leaned in ever so slightly and said, "Ah, yeah, you had a good orthodontist." Then he too smiled and leaned back. "Ortho, for straight or proper and *dox* from the word *doxa,* which means 'glory' or 'praise,' or even 'opinion,' like with the word *paradox.*"

"Opposing opinions?" I offered.

"Essentially," he said.

"And so orthodox means 'proper opinion?'"

Shep nodded and added, "Or 'proper praise.'"

"Okay," I said, suggesting we move on.

Shep recapped, "So if you were in good standing at an orthodox church, when you traveled you would let the clergy know and you would commune."

I noticed that my cup was empty and engaged the carafe to solve the problem. When I hit the rim I offered to top off Shep's. He accepted the offer, then said, "This is probably as good a time as any to excuse myself for a minute. I'll be right back."

Shep shifted to the edge of the booth's bench and stood up. I could tell his body was stiff and heard it crack as he stood. He sighed as he made a deliberate effort to stand taller than normal. He put his hands on the small of his back and pushed out a deep breath of relief. His spine popped as he did. He relaxed into his natural posture and tottered toward the restrooms. While he was gone I checked my phone. Nothing needed my attention so I pulled up my Notes app and typed in some reminders regarding what Shep had said so far.

When he returned, I could see he was in pain. With each step he tried to control the contortion of his face. When he saw that I was looking at him he forced a smile. As he squeaked back onto his padded seat he groaned and said, "The Church wants what God wants, for everyone to receive the life-giving, faith-strengthening, grace-giving gift of Communion. If you're a repentant, baptized believer who has confessed Christ before the world according to what Scripture says, then Jesus confesses you before His Father and you're welcomed to the family table." He was still settling into his spot in the booth; the vinyl seat squeaked with every move. "But unfortunately, there are heterodox churches that don't teach the truth of Scripture." He stopped in full realization that he dropped a new *dox* word on me.

I requested an explanation.

Shep said, "Dox."

And I echoed, "Praise."

Shep said, "Hetero."

I thought for a second and said, "As in *hetero*sexual?"

"That's right," Shep said. "Hetero means 'different.'"

"Heterosexuals are attracted to the different sex."

"And heterodox churches teach a different praise of God, a different *opinion* about who Jesus is or what He came for. Heterodox churches can be different on any number of things really," Shep said. "They teach their opinion, or the opinion of certain leaders, be it the current pastor or the founder of their denomination. This is instead of the proper, straight teaching of Scripture—they teach man's opinion instead of God's Word."

"And there were churches doing this in the first centuries?" I asked.

"Oh, yeah," Shep said with a resounding linger. "False teachers popped up right away. And they gathered quite a following, too."

I furrowed my brow in concern.

"In fact," Shep said, "the Nicene Creed, which came about in 325 AD, was the result of a council of clergymen who gathered to confront false teaching—heresy—with God's Word as it was properly revealed."

"I had no idea."

Shep took two short pulls from his pipe. "Once we had the Nicene Creed, the orthodox churches had a handy orthodox tool that they could use in their faithful administration of the Lord's Supper." He took another two puffs. "If someone didn't confess the creed, either he hadn't yet been taught or he held to a different opinion than that of the true—orthodox— Christian Church." The sweet smell of pipe tobacco filled the booth. "Either way, someone who wasn't in good standing or had a heterodox faith wasn't ready to receive Communion."

"So, I understand," I said. "The would-be communer—"

"Communicant," Shep said.

"The would-be *communicant* would say the Nicene Creed to prove he had an orthodox view of the Bible?"

"Yes. A creed is a confession of belief. *Credo* is Latin for 'I believe.' That's why we say the Nicene Creed in church on days when Communion is celebrated."

"To be honest, Shep, I remember saying the Nicene Creed at the closed Communion church, at least, I assume it was the Nicene Creed, but it felt weird. It, too, was a new experience for me."

Shep smiled and combed his fingers through his beard. I could tell his smile was the forebearer of something more.

"All right. Out with it. What's with the smile?" I said.

"I told you. You've been going to the wrong churches."

I smirked.

"You've never said the Nicene Creed?" He asked.

"Maybe. I'm trying to remember. I might have said something like it before. I don't know."

"Maybe you've confessed the Apostles' Creed. It's a little shorter, but also an orthodox creed."

"I'm not sure."

"The Apostles' Creed is a Baptismal creed. A simple confession that Christian converts would confess when they were baptized. Both became part of the Divine Service of orthodox churches."

We both took a drink. Shep let me think about what he had been saying. I had never realized there was so much to Communion. I had taken it now and then throughout my life. I always appreciated hearing about why it was special, about how it was done in remembrance of what Jesus did with His disciples before He went to the cross, but there was so much more to it than a special reenactment. In fact, Shep hadn't even talked about that. He mentioned the upper room, but then took me through the practice as it was in the Church, after Jesus instituted it.

As we sat drinking our coffee, my mind kept circling around Shep's claim that closed Communion was Christianity's historic practice. Other than its connection to Jesus, I never thought about it from an historical perspective. It made sense that it would have a history in the Church. So why was my experience with Communion not the same as that of the historic Church?

I chuckled to myself. My experience was *hetero*—different—from what the early Church had done. "I've been going to the wrong churches?" I whispered, but loud enough that Shep heard me. His eyes were sympathetic.

"I didn't mean to be rude," he said.

"No, you weren't. That's not what I meant." I waved my hand to the side as if to wipe away any notion that he offended me. "I didn't know anything about closed Communion before I bumped into you, but I've been to church plenty of times." I thought about it some more. "To be honest, it's a little troubling. You say I've been going to the wrong churches. You mean heterodox churches, don't you?"

"I do."

Shep looked at me. He was waiting for me to say something, but I was caught in thought. Closed Communion wasn't so much about restricting participation, but about teaching truth—orthodoxy.

The Family Table

BEFORE I could ask Shep another question, he asked me one. "When you've received Communion at the churches you're used to, did everybody commune?"

I had to think about that. "Um, I don't know," I said.

Shep let my answer sit for a second and then asked, "Can you walk me through how it went the last time you took Communion?"

"Oh, sure." I tried to recall what it was like. "The pastor talked about what it was, that Jesus told the disciples to do it in remembrance of Him."

"Did everyone come up to the altar to receive it?"

"No. We stayed seated and the ushers passed out trays of bread and grape juice," I said.

"Did everyone partake?"

"I think so." I thought about it. "If they wanted to." I thought about it some more. When the trays came by, it was a personal decision whether you wanted to take the bread and grape juice. I told Shep that.

"And that's what you were expecting at the closed Communion church?"

"Something similar, yeah."

"And like you said, it feels more welcoming for everyone present to be able to make that personal decision and take from the tray as it comes by, right?" Shep asked.

"Mmhmm," I said with a mouth full of lukewarm coffee.

Shep leaned the stem of his pipe against the edge of the ashtray and placed both his hands flat on the table, shoulder width apart. He sat up straight and said, "Why do you find that welcoming?"

"Huh?"

"What is welcoming about that way of doing Communion?" Shep pressed, flipping his palms off the table.

"I guess because..." I needed to think it through.

"Is it because no one says no?" Shep asked.

Shep relaxed his posture, rescued his pipe from the café ashtray, and took a drink of coffee.

I didn't answer. What was it that made the open Communion practice feel welcoming? Perhaps Shep had nailed it. I was allowed to participate in what was going on. I wasn't left out. Shut out like the five foolish virgins. Shut out like Adam and Eve.

"Communion is a *meal*," he said. "Right? We even call it the Lord's *Supper*. It was instituted by Jesus when He was observing the Passover meal with His disciples. Later, Scripture tells us that the Church in Corinth abused the meal. One guy would go hungry while another would get drunk. Each was eating his own meal, making a personal decision. What Jesus had established as a common, unifying meal, a corporate activity, had become individualized in a horrible way. In his first letter to the Corinthian church, St. Paul corrected their abuses." Shep stopped long enough to take a drink. "Communion is a sacred meal, but for a minute let's put that aside and consider other mealtime situations."

At the end of the table, next to the window, there was a cardboard display with pictures of desserts on it. Shep grabbed it. He acquainted himself with its contents and then handed it to me. As I looked at the dessert facing me, a pie called "Triple Chocolate Delight," Shep said, "What do you notice about those desserts?"

It was a three-sided display. I turned it to another side. There was a picture of "Grandma's Apple Pie." I flipped it over again. "Key Lime." "This café serves some delicious pies."

"Agreed," said Shep with a smile. "'Grandma's Apple' is close to the real deal. If that's the extent of their dessert menu, could you order a piece of cake?"

"No. Not if this is all they have."

"So, when the waitress comes by to check on us and you say, 'Can I get a piece of chocolate cake?' what is she going to say?"

"That they don't have it," I said.

"Right. She'll have to tell you no. The question is, is her 'no' unwelcoming?"

"Of course not. She can't give me something that's not on the menu."

"You're right again. But at least we can say that 'no' isn't always rude—unwelcoming, right?"

"Yeah," I said.

"God wasn't being rude when He told Adam and Eve 'no' to the tree of knowledge of good and evil, and then again when He closed the doors to Eden so that they wouldn't have to live with evil forever. If I asked the doctor if it was healthy to smoke a pipe, he wouldn't be rude to say no."

I said, "I get your point."

"While it might feel uncomfortable to be at a church where you're not able to participate in

Communion, it doesn't necessarily mean that the church isn't welcoming."

Shep was right, but the analogy didn't quite work. The café couldn't give me something it didn't have on hand. With closed Communion, I was denied what the church had, what everyone else received. I presented this critique to Shep.

"Excellent point," he said. "Let's say the café only had one thing on the menu. Pie. You came in and ordered pie and the waitress said no—"

"That wouldn't be welcoming," I interrupted and then added, "and a good way to get me to not come back." Shep grasped that my words were an allusion to the original frustration I had with closed Communion.

"Agreed. I'm sure this analogy has its faults—after all, a café is not a church—the café has customers it wants to keep happy, whereas the Church doesn't have customers and is focused on remaining faithful to God. But shortcomings aside, let's keep going with our comparison. What would you do if the waitress actually told you that you couldn't order one of those pies even though they have a bunch of them in the kitchen?"

"Well, first I'd ask her why not?"

"And I'd say you'd be right to expect an answer to that question." Shep motioned for the dessert display. I handed it to him and then he placed it back where it belonged. "You asked me about closed Communion, and I'm glad you did. I'm enjoying our conversation." Shep looked across the lobby at the hostess who was greeting a snow-covered couple who had just come in. "But did you ask the pastor of the closed Communion church why he refused to give you the Sacrament when he didn't have a problem giving it to others?"

I hesitated to answer. I hadn't asked the pastor about it at all. "No," I said.

Shep frowned. "Why not?"

"Good question," was my answer. "I was offended. I didn't want to talk to the pastor. He had upset me. The whole experience rubbed me the wrong way. I guess I wasn't interested in knowing more. I already knew I wasn't going to come back."

"In hindsight, would you say that it would've been better to ask for an explanation?"

"I get what you're saying," was as close to a yes as I could muster in the moment.

"Let's think about another mealtime situation," Shep said. "The family dinner table." He puffed on his pipe. "Say there's a family sitting down to eat dinner. Dad is there with mom and a whole table full of kids. The dinner table is in front of a big bay window. You're strolling down the sidewalk, look in the window, and see the family eating. Would you ever think of going into that house, sitting yourself down at the table as if you were one of the kids, and helping yourself to their food?"

"Of course not," I said.

"Why?"

"Because it's not my house, or my family."

Shep looked at me with an approving eye. "Like you pointed out with Jesus and the five foolish virgins, there's something to being known by the host of the meal. The family— dad—doesn't know you, so you wouldn't presume that you're welcome at his table without being invited, or at least first asking if it was okay." Shep's eyes shifted from me to the booth behind me, the one I had been seated at originally. The hostess was seating the cold couple who had just arrived. "I guess you're stuck with me now," he said with a chuckle. I glanced over my shoulder.

"I guess so," I said. "I hope you don't mind."

"Not at all. I'm glad I asked you to join me." Shep flashed his familiar smile.

"How's your coffee?" I said.

"Fill 'er up, please."

As I filled our cups, he continued. "Now, let's say you were invited to the table, would you go in and sit down?"

"Yeah."

"Of course you would. Why?"

"Because I was invited."

"Precisely. When you're invited, like with the wedding feast, you're welcome to sit and eat, just as if you were one of the family." He sipped his coffee. "Wow, that's hot!" He blew out in an attempt to cool down his lips. "I forgot it was the new stuff."

"So, we're back to having to be invited to take Communion?"

"Just like with the parable of the wedding feast," Shep said. "It's not surprising that you were taken aback by closed Communion, after all—and please don't take this the wrong way—but people these days feel entitled to things. Communion isn't for the entitled visitor. It's for the humble believer. Like we noticed with my analogy, church isn't a café. Not just anyone can come into the sanctuary and order up some bread and wine. The Lord's Supper is a family meal reserved only for its members. You need to be a believer to come to the Lord's Table."

I told Shep that he was giving me a lot of food for thought, to which he replied, "Well, maybe this will add a little more to your plate."

"What's that?"

"I don't know how it was when you were a kid, but when I was young I remember asking my parents' permission to have a friend over for dinner."

"Sure."

"And I remember being the one who was invited to a friend's house for dinner. Though it was dinner, just like at home, there was something unique about eating at someone else's house, right? My family did things our way, but my buddy's family did things their way. It was just dinner, but I remember sitting there wondering what to do. The freedom I had at home was gone. I knew when to dish up and how, but at my friend's house I waited until the food was offered to me, till his mom offered me some of this or some of that."

Shep took a sip of his coffee.

"That's humility. That's recognizing that you're a guest and even though you're welcome among them, until you're a part of the family, until you're treated like another one of the kids, you act like a guest." The old man tugged on his beard a little. "We understand this as kids, even if we're not aware of it. It's just good old-fashioned manners."

As Shep took me to his childhood days, I recalled my own. I remembered a time that I invited two friends to dinner without first seeing if it was okay with my mother. She was upset. It wasn't because she didn't like my friends or that she didn't want them to eat with us, but because it was unexpected. I had taken her for granted. It revealed a lack of appreciation for the person who prepared the meal. Likewise, someone had to prepare the Lord's Supper for everyone who would be in church on Sunday.

I couldn't help but think that in addition to everything the Bible said about the sacred meal, the closed Communion practice—purely on the practical level—was the practice my mom, and everyone who ever prepared a meal for others, would appreciate. It didn't take anyone for granted.

Allergies and Truth

AS I chewed on what I was learning about closed Communion, Shep and I talked about other stuff: holidays and family history, some local news, and again about the winter weather. It was nice, but all the while I was stuck on Communion. Eventually, I brought the conversation back around.

"Why is Communion so important?" I asked.

Shep looked at me like he was trying to see if there was something more behind my question.

I rephrased my inquiry. "It was important enough to the early Church to divide the heterodox from orthodox. Why?"

Still Shep looked at me with question marks in his eyes. When he spoke it was matter of fact, "Because it's where the Lord's body and blood are distributed to His people."

"Tell me more," I said. "Fill me in on the significance of the Lord's Supper."

"Okay," Shep replied, and then he started flipping through his Greek New Testament. "You know how I mentioned that Paul corrected the Corinthian abuses of the meal?"

"Yeah."

"Well..." It looked like he was almost to the page he was looking for. "As he told them their individualized practice despised God's Church and humiliated other Christians, he went into how the Sacrament was given to the Church and for what reason." Shep traced his finger over the words, "Here we go."

"Where are you in the New Testament?" I asked.

"This is 1 Corinthians 11. The abuses are addressed in verses 17 through 22."

"Thanks." I pulled out my phone and added the passage to my note.

Shep noticed and said, "I'm starting at verse twenty-three."

"Thanks."

"For I received from the Lord that which also I delivered to you, that the Lord Jesus on the night in which he was betrayed took bread. When he had given thanks, he broke it, and said, 'Take, eat. This is my body, which is broken for you. Do this in memory of me.' In the same way he also took the cup, after supper, saying, 'This cup is the new testament in my blood. Do this, as often as you drink, in memory of me.' For as often as you eat this bread and drink this cup, you proclaim the Lord's death until he comes."

He stopped, tapped his finger on the page, and repeated, "For as often as you eat this bread and drink this cup, you proclaim the Lord's death until he comes." Then he looked at me and said, "Communion is important because it's the proclamation of Christ's death. In other words, it's the proclamation of the Gospel."

"That's pretty important," I said with a chuckle.

"It's what the Church is all about," Shep said.

I held up my hand to make sure he wouldn't say anything more just yet. "Let me think out loud here." He nodded. "Communion is the Church proclaiming Jesus' death until He returns. It's the Church saying what John 3:16 says, that Jesus was given to save the world; like you said, that's what the Church is all about, saving people..." I took a second to find the right words. "So... if Jesus was given for the whole world, so that all who believe might be saved, why can't all who believe in Him take Communion at any church where its offered?"

"You are thinking out loud," Shep said with a caring grin.

"What do you mean?" I replied.

"You're thinking it through, but you forgot to consider that there is a difference in what the heterodox and orthodox believe, even though both say they're Christian. Or to take it back to one of the parables, if you would've asked the five foolish virgins if they believed in the Bridegroom before His return, they would've said yes, but their practice revealed they believed differently than the wise virgins."

I leaned back in thought.

Shep continued, "I should've read a little further in the text. Verse twenty-seven and following says, 'Therefore whoever eats this bread or drinks the Lord's cup in a way unworthy of the Lord will be guilty of the body and the blood of the Lord. But let a man examine himself, and so let him eat of the bread, and drink of the cup. For he who eats and drinks in an unworthy way eats and drinks judgment to himself, if he doesn't discern the Lord's body. For this reason, many among you are weak and sickly, and not a few have died. For if we discerned ourselves, we wouldn't be judged. But when we are judged, we are punished by the Lord, that we may not be condemned with the world.'"

"But wait," I said, again raising my hand to stop the conversation, "you just read it."

"What's that?" Shep asked.

"The part about a man examining himself. Paul says I need to examine *myself*. Doesn't that mean I should be able to decide for myself whether or not to take Communion?"

"I like how you think," Shep said through a wide-mouthed smile, and with his left index finger aimed at me. He wagged it and said, "You test what is said against the Word of God. Don't ever stop doing that."

I thanked him for the compliment and waited for his answer.

"Yes, we're to examine ourselves so that we eat of the bread and drink of the cup worthily. Paul said, 'Whoever, therefore, eats the bread or drinks the cup of the Lord in an unworthy manner will be guilty concerning the body and blood of the Lord.' The question we need to ask is, what does it mean to examine one's self?"

"I guess... making sure you're a good person—a Christian," I said.

Shep opened his mouth to speak, paused, thought for a second, and then said, "Well, you're half right. Examining yourself is reflecting on what it means to be a Christian, but that means recognizing that you're not a good person."

"How's that?" I asked.

"A pre-Communion examination is a confession of sins, reflecting on God's Word and seeing just how desperate you are for Jesus' salvation. Remember, Communion is the proclamation of Christ's death until he returns. Why did He die?"

"To save me from hell."

"And saving you from hell is saving you from your sins and the death you deserve because of them. That's what a self-examination entails. The Christian considers his sinfulness under God's holy Law and comes to the conclusion that his only hope is the Gospel—the death and resurrection of Jesus."

"That's right," I said. "But it says I'm to do this myself. That's the point closed Communion misses."

I took a drink.

"But it doesn't," Shep said. "How would anyone be able to examine himself under God's Law and rejoice in the Gospel unless pastors—the men God calls to be overseers of Christians—presented it to them?" Shep could see I was considering his words. "Holding onto an individualized self-examination not only puts a person back into the divisive realm of the abuses Paul addressed in 1 Corinthians, but it forgets that pastors are shepherds given by God specifically to guide people in matters of the Faith."

Shep pointed to his New Testament, "The very letter we're reading is evidence that God's people need shepherds to guide them in these things. In Romans, Paul says," Shep fanned the pages to his left, scanned the text, and read, "the Lord is Lord of all, and is rich to all who call on him. For, 'Whoever will call on the name of the Lord will be saved.' How then will they call on him in whom they have not believed? How will they believe in him whom they have not heard? How will they hear without a preacher? And how will they preach unless they are sent? As it is written: 'How beautiful are the feet of those who preach the Good News of peace, who bring glad tidings of good things!'" He slid past a number of words and then read, "So faith comes by hearing, and hearing by the word of God."

Shep raised his hand as I had, to hold the conversation where it was. "Hebrews 13 is also helpful." He flipped the pages back to the right. "Remember your leaders, men who spoke to you the word of God, and considering the results of their conduct, imitate their faith. Jesus Christ is the same yesterday, today, and forever. Don't be carried away by *various* and *strange* teachings," Shep held his place with his thumb and added, "different—heterodox—teachings." He continued reading, "For it is good that the heart be established by grace, not by food, through which those who were so occupied were not benefited. We have an altar from which those who serve the holy tabernacle have no right to eat." Then he said, "Did you catch that? Those who serve the tabernacle—Jewish unbelievers—don't have a right to eat at the Christian altar. Right here we have an example of closed Communion."

I nodded.

"Okay, let's keep reading. 'For the bodies of those animals, whose blood is brought into the holy place by the high priest as an offering for sin, are burned outside of the camp. Therefore Jesus also, that he might sanctify the people through his own blood, suffered outside of the gate. Let us therefore go out to him outside of the camp, bearing his reproach. For we don't have here an enduring city, but we seek that which is to come. Through him, then, let us offer up a sacrifice of praise to God continually, that is, the fruit of lips which proclaim allegiance to his name. But don't forget to be doing good and sharing, for with such sacrifices God is well pleased.'"

Again, Shep paused.

"Here's the passage I really wanted to bring to your attention." He looked down and started reading again, "'Obey your leaders and submit to them, for they watch on behalf of your souls, as those who will give account, that they may do this with joy, and not with groaning, for that would be unprofitable for you.'"

"You're saying that the reason we have pastors is so they can help us with our self-examination?" I said as I tried to wrap my mind around what I had just heard.

"Yes. Pastors are always watching over Jesus' flock, guiding them, teaching them, shepherding them."

Hence the nickname, Shep, I thought as I took another sip of coffee. After I swallowed I said, "I never thought this through, Shep. There is so much to Communion. It's more than just a nice event that happens at church on occasion."

"That's right," he said. "Let's go back to 1 Corinthians for a minute. You'll appreciate this."

"What's that?" I asked. I did a little seated hop and leaned forward.

"Remember what we read? 'For anyone who eats and drinks without discerning the body eats and drinks judgment on himself,' remember?"

I nodded and waited for Shep to elaborate on the text.

"Well, think about closed Communion as a way of protecting you from eating and drinking judgment on yourself."

"Okay, how so?"

Shep's answer took me by surprise. "Like a peanut allergy."

"Seriously?" I laughed. "What do you mean?"

"Do you have any food allergies?"

"Nope."

"Imagine having a severe peanut allergy. People who do are extra careful to make sure they don't eat anything that has even been processed in a factory where it could have come into contact with peanuts."

I recalled seeing something to that effect on candy bar labels and shared my familiarity with Shep.

"Right," he said. "It can be lethal if the allergy is bad enough."

"And how does this relate to pastors and closed Communion?" I said.

"I'm getting there," he said. "If the person who is allergic to peanuts isn't discerning about the food he eats, he could end up in the hospital, and really without treatment, he could die. Ultimately, it's up to him to examine what food he eats, but he finds it very helpful to be able to read the package and learn that the candy bar could've come in contact with peanuts, or as is his hope, that it was packaged in a peanut free facility. If that's the case, he's free to eat the food." Shep dumped the contents of his pipe bowl into the ashtray. "Closed Communion is how the Church helps us discern what we're eating."

"What do you mean, what we're eating?" I asked. "We're eating Communion."

"What is Communion?" Shep said.

"It's bread and grape juice that represents Jesus' body and blood," I said.

Shep said, "It's more than that." He could tell I didn't follow. He offered an explanation. "Scripture teaches that in the Lord's Supper the bread and wine don't just represent the body and blood of Jesus, but that they *are* the *actual* body and blood of Jesus."

"What?"

"Not all churches teach that."

"Are we back to orthodox and heterodox churches?" I asked.

Shep smiled his affirmation. "Churches that believe, teach, and confess that the bread and wine are just what Jesus said they are, His body and blood, speak truth and anyone who believes it is, well, according to our analogy, eating a candy bar processed in a nut free factory."

"And what do heterodox churches say?" I asked.

"They're not all the same, but it's common for today's 'Evangelical' churches to teach that the bread and wine *represent* Christ's body and blood."

"Which is like a candy bar being processed in a factory with peanuts?"

"Yes," Shep said. "One is good, and one only looks good, but in actuality, it's extremely dangerous."

"For the allergic person?" I said.

"Yes, and we're all allergic to what's not true," Shep said, and then added, "Closed Communion assists people in discerning truth. If a Christian goes to a church that practices open Communion, he could be receiving food that has come in contact with what is not true. It would otherwise be good for him, but because it's in a factory open to 'peanuts' it could hurt him."

Our coffee cups were cooling off so Shep warmed them up with a little more java from the carafe. The waitress was behind me taking the order of the couple who were seated in my old booth.

Shep pulled out his tobacco tin again and said, "The peanut allergy is a way to understand that we can take Communion to our detriment if we don't discern that we're sinners in need of a savior. And while it's also a way of coming to appreciate that closed Communion is not the

Church trying to keep people out, but rather a faithful practice for the health and well-being of believers and would-be believers, it's a little sterile."

"Sterile?"

As the waitress walked by she checked on our coffee reserves. We had a couple cups to go before we needed any more. An appreciation for the unlimited café coffee flashed through my mind.

"The analogy doesn't hit quite as hard as Scripture," Shep said.

"Let's hear it," I said.

"Okay, 1 Corinthians 10 says, 'I speak as to wise men. Judge what I say. The cup of blessing which we bless—'"

"Communion," I interrupted.

Shep continued, "'Isn't it a sharing of the blood of Christ? The bread which we break, isn't it a sharing of the body of Christ? Because there is one loaf of bread, we, who are many, are one body; for we all partake of the one loaf of bread. Consider Israel according to the flesh. Don't those who eat the sacrifices participate in the altar? What am I saying then? That a thing sacrificed to idols is anything, or that an idol is anything? But I say that the things which the Gentiles sacrifice, they sacrifice to demons, and not to God, and I don't desire that you would have fellowship with demons. You can't both drink the cup of the Lord and the cup of demons. You can't both partake of the table of the Lord, and of the table of demons. Or do we provoke the Lord to jealousy? Are we stronger than he?'"

"Ah, cup of demons," I said. "Yeah, that hits a little harder than a peanut allergy."

"God doesn't mess around when it comes to His Church. To share the same cup and same bread is to be in fellowship with others, to be in *communion* with them in the Lord. If you belong to a church that doesn't teach the Truth of God's Word, but something different, even if you don't know it, you're not exactly participating in the same cup and same bread as the orthodox Church, are you?"

"I guess not," I said, "But does belonging to a heterodox denomination mean I'm partaking of the table of demons?"

"Intentionally? No. But those who know they're allergic to what's not true, to the lies of demons, are diligent not to let the demonic allergens enter the facility of truth." Shep started the process of reloading his pipe. "There are out-and-out pagans, and there are those who have somehow, someway let pagan doctrine and practice creep into their confession. In keeping with our analogy, there are peanuts and that which has come in contact with peanuts. The Church does not allow paganism—the table of demons—and it guards itself against what's been contaminated by paganism. It aims to keep everyone healthy. In this way, closed Communion also assists the confused Christian by declaring that not all churches are the same. Just like not all food factories are the same."

I had been attending heterodox churches and didn't even know I was learning something other than what Scripture taught. It was a bold statement, but I could see the truth, or at least I was beginning to see it.

"Shep, according to our analogy, I'd say I've been in contact with what I'm allergic to for quite some time now." I laughed and said, "You might want to call an ambulance."

He smiled and played along. "Are you going into anaphylactic shock?"

"I might be!"

The Medicine of Immortality

WE both had a laugh at my lighthearted request for an ambulance to treat my allergic reaction to false teaching. Shep's was a reserved laugh, like he wanted to laugh louder, but stifled it because he thought it would be inappropriate. It was a comforting laugh. The added sense of strain reassured me that it was okay to be happy, to smile, to laugh. It was like the seriousness of life was restricting him, and he was trying to break free, like he longed for a time and place of pure happiness where no one would take themselves too seriously and everyone could laugh as loud as they wanted.

He told me going to an orthodox church would bring healing and that it was good to view the Church like a hospital for the sickly sinner.

After the moment passed Shep said, "Your request for medical attention reminds me of what Ignatius of Antioch said."

"Englasius of Anti-what?"

He laughed a little more. "Ignatius of Antioch lived in the first and early second centuries and was a disciple of the apostle John."

"The apostles had disciples?" I asked.

"You know they did," he said. "How else do you think the Gospel spread? A disciple is a follower, a student of a teacher," Shep said.

"Oh. Yeah, that makes sense."

Shep had prepared his pipe for another smoke and puffed on as we talked. A few plumes rolled away from the pipe like smoke from the stack on an old train. "Ignatius became the bishop of Antioch, and eventually he was martyred in Rome, but not before he could write some letters. In one of them, a letter to the Church in Ephesus, he instructed the

Christians there to be united in obedience to the bishops and pastors, breaking the one bread of Communion in unity. Interestingly enough, he called it the medicine of immortality."

"An epipen for the allergic?" I said in jest.

"That's right. He said it was an antidote for the dying; medicine to prevent us from dying, so we would live forever with Jesus."

"You're kidding."

Shep smiled and said, "Not at all."

"Hey, your peanut allergy analogy really works."

"Thanks. It didn't come from nowhere."

Before Shep could go on I asked another question. "I get the wedding feast parable and the family dinner table comparisons. I mean, it's food we're talking about. But why medicine?"

He smiled. "Another great question from my untimely disciple."

I smiled back.

He said, "The answer gets us back to what Jesus says about the bread and wine, that they're His body and blood."

Shep could see that I didn't quite follow.

"We already read it in 1 Corinthians, but how about we look at it in Matthew?" He walked his fingers over the pages like a miniature circus performer walking on a barrel. The pages rolled out from under his digits until he arrived at the Gospel of Matthew. "This is an easy passage to remember, Matthew 26:26."

I punched the Scripture address into my phone with the other notes.

Shep read, "As they were eating, Jesus took bread, gave thanks for it, and broke it. He gave to the disciples, and said, 'Take, eat; this *is* my body.' He took the cup, gave thanks, and gave to them, saying, 'All of you drink it, for this *is* my blood of the new covenant, which is poured out for many for the remission of sins.'"

The woman sitting behind me sneezed. Her husband and Shep said, "bless you," in unison. She sniffled and thanked them. The winter night wasn't doing her cold any favors.

Shep continued. "The bread and wine are truly the body and blood of Christ," he said. "Food? Yes, but not just food. Food that gives life. Isn't that what medicine is, if you think about it? Pills are swallowed and once in our systems they heal us. If the ailment is bad enough, the right pill will prevent death."

"Oh, I see."

"It's easy to see, isn't it?" He exhaled smoke with his words. "But, it's good to remember the Corinthian Christians."

"What about them?"

"How Paul said their abuses were causing them to be sick, and that some had even died because of it."

"Ah," I said, as if a lightbulb was turned on over my head. "They abused the medicine."

"That's right, medicine is good for the person who needs it, but can be lethal to someone who doesn't, someone who misuses it."

"But don't we all need the medicine of immortality?" I asked.

"Oh, yeah," Shep exclaimed, "but not everybody is ready to receive it."

I was puzzled. "Who wouldn't be ready to receive it? Unbelievers?"

"Indeed. Anyone who doesn't believe the food is what Jesus said it is: His body and blood. Anyone who doesn't believe that he is what God's Word says he is: a sinner. Anyone who—"

"The heterodox," I said.

Shep pulled smoke from his pipe. "That's right."

I tipped my cup for a drink.

Shep said, "It's a blessing to the repentant sinner who trusts in God's Word. It's a curse to the unrepentant. It brings judgment on them."

"Hence closed Communion?" I inquired.

"That's right," Shep said, "Closed Communion is the faithful way of administering the medicine of immortality. Just like a good doctor doesn't administer a drug to a patient without first knowing his condition, a good pastor doesn't administer the medicine of immortality without first knowing something about the faith of the recipient."

"But what if they believe everything Scripture says, except maybe one or two things?" I asked. "Are they abusing Communion if they believe it's Christ's body and blood, and they're repentant of their sins, but, I don't know, they don't believe some less important things?"

Shep smiled at me, streaming smoke from his nostrils. Once it was expelled he said, "First, everything Scripture says is important. Second, you can't trust God in one article of faith and deny Him in another. The Bible's teaching is singular. God is everything in each article of the Faith and all of them are united in Him."

"So...?"

"So, to expand our comparison to include all of God's Word, if the effects of a medicine are X, Y, and Z, that's what it'll do when you take it, X, Y, and Z. It's dangerous to say you believe X and Y while denying Z. Know what I mean?"

"I think so."

"I'm sure you've picked up a prescription from the pharmacist before, right?"

I nodded.

"When it's a new prescription what does the pharmacist do when you arrive to pick it up?"

"He tells you what it's all about."

"Right. There's a consultation. You have to be instructed on the ins and outs of the medicine before you can take it," Shep said.

It made perfect sense. I wouldn't want to take a medicine I didn't know about. "Shep," I said, "This is the most I've ever learned about Communion. Why don't pastors teach that much about it?"

He put up his hand. "Many don't, but be honest, are you a regular church-goer? Do you go to Bible Study every Sunday?" He knew the answers to his questions before he asked them.

I shook my head.

"While your observation is true, be careful not to put all the blame on pastors if you don't know what they teach week in and week out."

"Fair enough," I said, "But you said my observation is true."

"Yes. You're right. God's messengers would do well to spend more time teaching about the

Sacrament. It's central to the Faith and was instituted by Christ Himself. Together with God's Word and Baptism, it's the means by which God bestows His grace on us sinners."

"It's too bad pastors aren't under the same sort of scrutiny doctors are," I said.

"How's that?" asked Shep.

"If pastors feared getting hit with a malpractice lawsuit, they'd probably take their job of administering the Sacrament a little more seriously."

"I bet you're right," Shep said, "but wouldn't you think the fear of God would outweigh the threat of a lawsuit?"

"True, and yet so many pastors seem to administer the medicine of immortality recklessly."

Shep shook his head in disdain. "True."

The woman behind me sneezed again and the echo of God's blessings was heard once more. I checked the status of the carafe. Nearly empty. I twisted the lid off and placed it sideways on top so that the waitress would see we needed some more.

Shep said, "Though it doesn't involve eating food, you could compare the Eucharist to receiving a blood transfusion."

"What did you call it?" I asked.

"The Eucharist," he said, "It's another name for the Lord's Supper. It's from the Greek and means *thanksgiving*."

That term was new to me, but it wasn't the point of what Shep had said, so I didn't get us off track by asking for more information. Instead, I encouraged him to explain the comparison between the Sacrament and a blood transfusion. He started by mentioning that they both deal with the giving of blood by one person for the benefit of others. But the main substance of the comparison rested in the care required for a blood transfusion to be a healing activity.

"If you take Communion without discerning the body and blood of Christ, you drink judgment upon yourself. That's a bad thing. Serious. Death. But if in preparation for the Lord's Supper, you examine yourself and discern the body and blood of Jesus—if you repent of your sin, trust that Christ is really present in the meal to forgive your sins, and desire to change your sinful ways by the power of the Holy Spirit—then receiving Jesus' body and blood brings life. It's like Jesus has a certain blood type that only believers share."

He continued, "When someone needs a transfusion, the medical staff has to first examine the patient's blood type. Not all blood types are interchangeable. If you were to receive a blood type that wasn't compatible with yours, it would make you sick and could kill you. Receiving Christ's blood in a supernatural blood transfusion is nothing to take lightly, and what a blessing it is to attend a church where the pastors, like doctors and nurses, take it seriously, permitting the procedure for those who need it and restricting it from those who would suffer from it."

The woman in the booth behind me sniffled and then blew her nose loudly. The interruption allowed Shep to turn the conversation around. "Pastors who take Communion seriously don't just keep it from non-members, they're also diligent to distribute it and restrict it among the members of the parish according to each person's faith. If a baptized believer develops an unrepentant attitude toward sin, the pastor, like an emergency room doctor, may need to withhold Communion, so the parishioner doesn't add injury to illness."

"Oh, like how hospitals restrict how much pain medicine a patient can self-administer with the clicky thing?" I said.

"Exactly like that!" was Shep's reply. "Likewise, a pastor would be guilty of malpractice if he withheld the medicine of immortality from someone who was ready to receive it, someone who was in dire need of its healing."

"Does that happen?" I asked.

"Sadly, it can. A doctor can abuse medicine both by giving it and withholding it. Pastors stand in the place of the Great Physician in the parish they serve, which means they try their hardest through study of God's Word and life with their parishioners, to know when to administer the medicine and when to withhold it. Like with healthcare, errors in judgment can and do happen in the ministry. Pastors are sinners, too."

I thought about Shep's words as he lifted his coffee and held it between both hands, as if to warm his palms through the ceramic cup. The goal was to heal repentant sinners. I ran that statement by Shep. He agreed without hesitation and mentioned that the Lord's Supper was all about strengthening the Christian's faith. When I asked him to elaborate, he asked me if I had ever been to a gym.

Exercising the Faith Muscle

HAVE I ever been to the gym? Of course. "Actually, I still have a membership to the gym in the old part of town," I said. "Do you know the one?"

Shep nodded.

"It's a great facility."

"I'm sure it is," Shep said. "The Lord's Supper is a lot like going to the gym."

I smiled at the old man. He had so many wonderful ways of explaining the ins and outs of the Lord's Supper, but I doubted he spent a lot of time working on his physique. I felt comfortable enough to rib him a little. "Do you spend a lot of time at the gym, Shep?"

He smiled. "Not these days, but I do spend a lot of time at the Lord's Table."

"You do?"

"I do."

"How often do you take Communion?"

"Every Sunday."

"Every Sunday?!"

"Every Sunday."

I had only taken Communion a handful of times. Granted I wasn't the most regular church goer, but I had never imagined taking it every single week. As a pastor, Shep would've been at church a lot more than I had been, but he wasn't one anymore, and he still took Communion every Sunday.

My impression was that it was a special event offered every once in a while. With much enthusiasm Shep confirmed that it was an event more special than any other, and that as a Christian he was blessed to receive it as often as he could. When I asked why, he explained that God took on flesh and dwelt among man to serve us. He did that on the cross where He died, taking away our sins. Communion, Shep said, was the way that His Divine Service was given from the cross to His Church.

"People go to the gym," Shep said, "to get—or stay—fit, right?"

"That's the goal," I said.

"That's why people commune as well. To strengthen their faith." He sipped from his cup. "The Communion rail is the place where Christians exercise their faith muscle."

"Their faith muscle?"

Shep bent his left arm as if he was flexing his bicep. "Mmhmm."

"Okay, explain," I said.

"Gladly. What happens when you take Communion?"

I didn't know what he was getting at. Was he talking spiritually? I couldn't put that into words very well. I tried, but the right description eluded me. He couldn't be talking physically, we already talked about my experiences taking Communion. I asked him to clarify.

"At the churches where you've communed, the ushers passed trays of bread and wine down the—"

"Not wine. Grape juice," I said.

"Grape juice," Shep repeated. "Okay, you eat the bread and drink the grape juice. What's going—"

"I'm sorry, I don't mean to keep interrupting you, but your church uses wine?"

"It does," Shep said.

"But drunkenness is a sin."

"Yes."

"So why does your church do something that encourages drinking?"

Shep stroked his beard and said, "Our Lord used wine when He instituted His Supper, which He says is His new testament. Are you familiar with what a testament is?"

"You mean, like when someone leaves a last will and testament?" I said.

"Exactly! That's what the Lord's Supper is. Jesus laid out what He wanted us to do after He died. And just like we can't change the last will and testament of our dead relatives, we can't change the last will and testament of our Lord. He used wine, so we use wine."

"That doesn't make any sense," I said. "Why would Jesus have His disciples drink wine if it's a sin to get drunk?"

"A person can have a drink without getting drunk. While it can be abused, wine is a blessing from God given to gladden man's heart."

It actually did make sense. "So why do some churches use grape juice?" I asked.

"Misunderstanding. A desire to avoid temptation maybe. A misguided sense of pietism. There are a number of reasons really."

I scratched my head.

Shep continued, "We started talking about Communion by considering it as a wedding rehearsal, remember?"

I nodded, still in thought.

"Well, Jesus attended a wedding at the beginning of His ministry, and while He was there the wine ran out. His first miracle was turning water into wine, which, as it turns out, was even recognized as the good stuff."

"Jesus made *top-shelf* alcohol?!"

With a wide-mouthed smile and a sparkle in his eye, Shep said, "Would you expect anything less from your God?"

"I guess not."

"The dress rehearsal of Communion is for the greatest of all weddings. The marriage feast of the Lamb, when He is united with His bride, the Church." As Shep finished his sentence, he retrieved his Hebrew Old Testament and started searching for a passage. "Listen to this from Isaiah. He's talking about the work of our Lord and that day when sin will be no more, the day we've been talking about as the marriage feast of the Lamb." Shep found where he wanted to start reading. "In this mountain, Yahweh of Armies will make all peoples a feast of fat things, a feast of choice *wines*, of fat things full of marrow, of well refined choice *wines*." Shep looked at me and said, "Wine isn't bad. And on top of all that, the whole unfermented grape juice option wasn't a thing until Welches in the nineteenth century."

"Really?"

"Really. There wasn't a Christian on earth that received non-alcoholic grape juice in Communion for the first 1800 some odd years of Jesus' 2000-year-old Sacrament."

I didn't know why exactly the churches I had attended used grape juice, but Shep went on to tell me that his pastor wanted him and everyone who received Communion to be sure they were receiving the forgiveness of sins that Jesus promised, which was delivered with His body and blood in, with, and under the bread and *wine* of the Lord's Supper. That brought us back to his question about what was going on with me when I took Communion.

He said one of the things that divided the heterodox from the orthodox was whether Christ was really present in the sacred meal. He said, "Some churches teach that the bread and wine represent Christ's body and blood, but the orthodox Church has always taught what Jesus said, namely, that it *is* His body and blood."

"But it's clearly not His human flesh and blood," I said.

"Really?"

"How can it be?"

"That is the mystery," Shep said, "and that is why going to the Communion rail is like going to the gym. It strengthens your faith like lifting weights strengthens your biceps." He smiled and feigned a bicep flex again.

"So, you're saying that the fact that it isn't actually Jesus' body and blood is what builds your faith that it is His body and blood?" I asked.

"Close. But it is *actually* His body and blood. My physical senses don't grasp it, true, and as a fallen creature they even deceive me as I'm kneeling at the rail, but Christ promised me that it is His body and blood. Christians take Him at His word, and what one finds is that believing what He says, instead of believing fallen perception, strengthens the faith."

I sipped my coffee, and Shep used his pipe to fill the vicinity with a thick grey cloud. He looked at me like he could see my brain working extra hard to sort through the new information.

"Consider all this in light of two other passages of Scripture," Shep said.

"Okay."

"First, what Jesus said to Thomas. Thomas had told the other disciples that he wouldn't believe Jesus had been raised from the dead unless he could touch the Lord's body. He wanted to see His flesh as evidence of His real presence." Shep was back in his New Testament.

"What did Jesus say to him?" I asked.

Shep started reading John 20:26, "Jesus came, the doors being locked, and stood in the middle, and said, 'Peace be to you.' Then he said to Thomas, 'Reach here your finger, and see my hands. Reach here your hand, and put it into my side. Don't be unbelieving, but believing.' Thomas answered him, 'My Lord and my God!' Jesus said to him, 'Because you have seen me, you have believed. Blessed are those who have not seen, and have believed.'"

Shep took a drink.

"Our Lord does the incomprehensible. He enters a room though a locked door. He is bodily present with the disciples, the Church, and for Thomas He reveals His real presence. Then what did He say? 'Blessed are those who have not seen, and have believed.'"

"Whoa! I never knew Doubting Thomas had anything to do with Communion."

"Everything in Scripture has to do with one thing, salvation in Christ Jesus. We're saved by grace, and there are specific ways God bestows that grace upon us. His Word and Sacraments: Baptism and Communion. Scripture is all about the grace of God in Christ Jesus. It's all about how God bestows His grace on us."

"What's the other Scripture passage?" I asked.

Shep turned his pages.

"Back in 1 Corinthians, this time in chapter, um, thirteen, verse... twelve, St. Paul says, 'For now we see in a mirror, dimly, but then face to face. Now I know in part, but then I will know fully, even as I was also fully known.'"

"So," I began slowly, thinking through what I heard, "the bread and wine are Christ's body and blood even though we can't see it, and it just looks like bread and grape—err, wine?"

"That's about right. See, Christians are humble. We acknowledge that in all things God's ways are higher than our ways. We're not playing pretend or anything like that. When we say the bread *is* the body of Christ, we still see bread, we still taste bread, but we trust Christ's word, and He said 'take eat, this *is* my body.' The Lord's Table is *the* place where we exercise our faith."

"Like going to the gym?"

"Right. It's not that we don't exercise our faith throughout our daily lives too, but Communion is an intentional trip to the gym to work out, to get stronger in the Faith. It's where we trim the fat of sin, and learn to rely on God."

"Because each time you receive Jesus' body and blood, how did you say it?"

"In, with, and under—"

"Yeah, in, with, and under the bread and wine?"

"You got it," Shep said.

I smiled at Shep and flexed my arm. "If you take Communion every week, you must be able to lift a ton."

He restrained a laugh and with a huge grin said, "And now is a good time to talk about not getting carried away with analogies."

I understood what he was saying, but I could tell that he was anxious to make sure he was being clear. He said, "Please understand that the work of the Christian is to believe. That's what we're given to do. And the ability to do that is actually given to us by God, so even that work is not our own. It's all God. The point of this analogy is to say that at the Lord's Supper the Christian exercises his faith muscle by trusting, or believing the words of Christ to be true. Faith is lived out in Communion with God."

"And what happens if I don't believe the bread and wine are really Jesus' body and blood? Do I not get to take Communion at a closed Communion church?" I asked.

"Would a weight trainer let you do a particular exercise without first teaching you how to do it?" was Shep's reply.

"No."

"No. That would be irresponsible. Dangerous even. You could hurt yourself. Closed Communion churches don't want you to hurt yourself. They want you to grow stronger in your faith, and so they teach first."

I Am the Bread

THE couple sitting in the booth behind me finished their meal, paid their bill, and left while Shep and I continued our conversation. We weren't showing the slightest sign of drawing our excursion into the Lord's Supper to a close, when the waitress came by and informed us that the café would be closing soon.

I had learned so much already and wanted to know more. In all honesty, Shep was the kind of person whose disposition invited conversation. To talk with him was to feel appreciated and likewise to grow in an appreciation of things previously unknown.

As we worked on finishing the remainder of the carafe's offerings, Shep explained that the words Jesus used to institute His Supper—this *is* my body and this *is* my blood—had proven to be a real stumbling block for many people, which led to a lot of division among Christians.

"Too bad Jesus didn't use different words," I said.

"He was intentional about the words He used," Shep said.

"I know, but I don't imagine Jesus wanted to cause division."

"No, of course not. God is about unity. But Jesus did say He didn't come to bring peace, but a sword."

"How's that?"

"The word of truth unites those who believe it, but some reject it."

Shep dumped his pipe out. He took his time inspecting the bowl as he said, "The division we see today is reminiscent of the division believers witnessed in Jesus' day. It grieves the Church that people don't trust His Word."

From there he took me to 1 Corinthians 1 and said, "Listen to this as you think about Communion and Christ's words of institution." He offered brief and intermittent commentary as he read: "'For the word of the cross'—that's the Gospel of Jesus—'is foolishness to those who are dying'—those who don't believe in Jesus—'but to us who are saved it is the power of God. For it is written, "I will destroy the wisdom of the wise, I will bring the discernment of the discerning to nothing."'"

He wanted me to notice that Jesus Himself is the reason people don't believe in Him, that not believing the bread and wine are actually the body and blood of the Lord is akin to what Paul said.

I cut in, "The wisdom of the wise says it's just bread and wine, not body and blood?"

"That's right. Their wisdom says that we can discern with our senses that it's not flesh and blood. But human reason and senses are used in service to what God's Word says." He read on. "Where is the wise? Where is the scribe? Where is the lawyer of this world? Hasn't God made foolish the wisdom of this world?" He presented a summary. "The wisdom of this world says dead people stay dead, yet Jesus died and rose from the grave three days later, revealing the foolishness of the world's so-called wisdom."

I signaled my understanding with a nod.

Shep continued reading, "For seeing that in the wisdom of God, the world through its wisdom didn't know God, it was God's good pleasure through the foolishness of the preaching to save those who believe." He looked at me and said, "The preaching of the crucified and resurrected Jesus, who has given and shed His body and blood for us," his eyes went back to the page, "For Jews ask for signs, Greeks seek after wisdom, but we preach Christ crucified; a stumbling block to Jews, and foolishness to Greeks, but to those who are called, both Jews and Greeks, Christ is the power of God and the wisdom of God. Because the foolishness of God is wiser than men and the weakness of God is stronger than men."

I asked him to stop reading for a second, waited for my words to catch up with my thoughts, and then said, "The foolishness and weakness of God, that's Christ being crucified for the forgiveness of sins, which is wiser and stronger than the way the world does things because mankind keeps sinning? Is that about right?"

"You've got a good noodle up there," Shep said, pointing at my head. "And so what would be the relationship to the Lord's Supper?"

I bit my lower lip in thought before saying, "The Lord's Supper is how the cross is distributed to those who believe in Jesus—that He died for them. So... it's part of the foolishness and weakness of God that is stronger than the wisdom and strength of men."

Shep smiled and slapped the table with enthusiasm. He nodded his head with such excited approval that he looked like a bobble head. I chuckled, and then when he settled down he read some more, "You see your calling, brothers, that not many are wise according to the flesh, not many mighty, and not many noble; but God chose the foolish things of the world that he might put to shame those who are wise." Once again, he stopped and added a comment. "We can understand Christ's real presence in Communion according to this passage. The world sees the Church's belief as foolish, and that is what shames them."

"They think we're foolish, which reveals their foolishness?" I said.

Shep nodded and read some more. "'God chose the weak things of the world, that he might put to shame the things that are strong; and God chose the lowly things of the world'—*like bread and wine*—'and the things that are despised, and the things that are not, that he might bring to nothing the things that are: that no flesh should boast before God. Because of him, you are in Christ Jesus, who was made to us wisdom from God, and righteousness and sanctification, and redemption: that, accordingly as it is written, "He who boasts, let him boast in the Lord.""'

After Shep finished reading he circled back around and said, "Jesus is a stumbling block and foolishness to unbelievers. They look at the historical account of a man dying on a cross, and even before they consider the miraculous, almighty power of God, they dismiss it. To the world, death is defeat, not victory. The heterodox person, who says Christ can't truly be present at the Lord's Supper because our senses tell us we're eating bread and drinking wine, is displaying the same disbelief. The Christian trusts God even though he can't always intellectually comprehend how He does what He does."

"It's about faith," I said.

"Yes. A reasonable faith can believe God does incomprehensible things in our lives because He has proven Himself trustworthy and capable."

"What was the first thing you read there?"

He traced his finger back to where he had started reading. "'For the word of the cross is foolishness to those who are dying but to us who are saved it is the power of God.' 1 Corinthians 1:18."

"And Communion is the word of the cross, to be sure. It's all about Jesus dying on the cross for me," I said, more to myself than to Shep, but loud enough for him to hear.

He flipped to another book of the Bible. "The Holy Spirit inspired Peter to say something similar to Paul."

"Really?"

Shep nodded and read, "Because it is contained in Scripture, 'Behold, I lay in Zion a chief cornerstone, chosen, and precious: He who believes in him will not be disappointed.' For you who believe therefore is the honor, but for those who are disobedient, 'The stone which the builders rejected, has become the chief cornerstone,' and, 'a stone of stumbling, and a rock of offense.' For they stumble at the word, being disobedient, to which also they were appointed."

"It's all about believing the Word, not rejecting it," I said.

"That's it," Shep said.

"What passage was that?"

"1 Peter 2:6-8."

"It makes sense," I said, "That's the whole reason Jesus came to earth and did all His miracles. Isn't that what the Old Testament stories are all about, the Israelites believing Moses..." My words trailed off as I tried to recollect the Bible stories I learned as a kid.

Shep concluded my thought, "And the prophets. Yes, that's why we refer to Christianity as the Faith. It's all about believing God's Word, which we have good reason to do. It's about who we trust: God or ourselves. We either believe what *He* says or what *we* think."

"I guess it would be easier if we had Jesus right in front of us the way the disciples did," I said.

Shep smiled. "You would think so, wouldn't you?"

I nodded.

Shep smiled some more. "Jesus taught this and people turned away from Him."

"What?! You've got to be kidding."

"I wish I were. Listen to this." He thumbed his way to another spot in the New Testament. "John 6, if you want to put it in your phone." I did. "Jesus has just fed five thousand men by working a miracle with food."

"Oh, with, um, the loaves of bread and the fish."

"That's right. The food was unending until everyone ate their fill."

I could tell Shep was skimming the words to find what he was looking for. "After feeding His followers, He withdrew to be by Himself. Then He walked on water to the disciples in a boat." Shep found his spot. "Here we go. The people are seeking him and they get into this conversation with Him about food. Listen to this, Jesus told them, 'Don't work for the food which perishes, but for the food which remains to eternal life, which the Son of Man will give to you. For God the Father has sealed him.'" Shep looked at me. "These guys want to know what they have to do in order to do God's work. Jesus says to them, 'This is the work of God, that you believe in him whom he has sent.'"

"Like you said earlier, the work of the Christian is to believe?"

"Yep. So then these followers of Jesus who before had been miraculously fed with the bread and the fish said to Him, 'What then do you do for a sign, that we may see, and believe you? What work do you do?'"

"Really? The miraculous feeding wasn't sign enough?"

Shep smiled and continued, "They said, 'Our fathers ate the manna in the wilderness.'" Shep asked if I was familiar with the Exodus. I told him I remembered learning about it as a kid, at which point he encouraged me to not just rely on my childhood, but to dive into Scripture as an adult. Then he returned us to what Jesus' followers said. "As it is written, 'He gave them bread out of heaven to eat.'"

I said, "God kind of has a thing for bread, doesn't He?"

"You could certainly say that," Shep said. "But is that surprising? After all, God shows us His grace through His Word and Sacraments. Baptism and Communion, and the elements used in them—water, bread, and wine—are everywhere in the Bible. And I believe that is for good reason: so that we always have His grace and how He shows it to us on our minds as we read, mark, and inwardly digest His Word." He took a sip of coffee and said, "Keep listening. Jesus said, 'Most certainly, I tell you, it wasn't Moses who gave you the bread out of heaven, but my Father gives you the true bread out of heaven. For the bread of God is that which comes down out of heaven, and gives life to the world.' They said therefore to him, 'Lord, always give us this bread.'"

With his index finger pinched between the pages of his Bible he said, "Now here it is, are you ready?"

"Of course," I said with a grin.

He opened back to his spot and read, "Jesus said to them, 'I am the bread of life. He who comes to me will not be hungry, and he who believes in me will never be thirsty. But I told you that you have seen me, and yet you don't believe.'" When he finished reading he pointed at me and said, "Just like you said. They have

Jesus with them, you'd think that would make it easier to believe, yet they still don't."

"That's crazy," I said.

"I know, but disbelief runs deep."

I was shaking my head in my own disbelief, thinking about what it would be like to have Jesus right in front of me, to have Him feed me, and yet not believe His Word when Shep said, "There's more. Jesus said the will of His Father who sent Him was 'that everyone who sees the Son, and believes in him, should have eternal life' and be raised up on the last day by Jesus."

"What does that mean exactly?" I said.

"That if you look to the cross and believe that Jesus gave His life for you, you'll live with Him forever."

"Well, that makes me want to exercise my faith muscle."

Shep smiled and said, "For sure." He held up a finger and went back to the text, "The Jews therefore murmured concerning him, because he said, 'I am the bread which came down out of heaven.'" Shep pulled his head up and said, "You see, they knew Jesus. He was Joseph's son, just a regular guy as far as they were concerned. Jesus tells them..." Shep's eyes searched for his place, "It is written in the prophets, 'They will all be taught by God.' Therefore everyone who hears from the Father, and has learned, comes to me. Not that anyone has seen the Father, except he who is from God. He has seen the Father. Most certainly, I tell you, he who believes in me has eternal life. I am the bread of life. Your fathers ate the manna in the wilderness, and they died. This is the bread which comes down out of heaven, that anyone may eat of it and not die. I am the living bread which came down out of heaven. If anyone eats of this bread, he will live forever. Yes, the bread which I will give for the life of the world is my flesh."

When Shep looked up my eyes were as wide as the mouth of our coffee cups. "'I am the bread of life! The bread which I will give is my flesh!' There it is."

Shep's ever present grin was wide and welcomed my enthusiasm. "Keep listening," he said. "The Jews therefore contended with one another, saying, 'How can this man give us his flesh to eat?' Jesus therefore said to them, 'Most certainly I tell you, unless you eat the flesh of the Son of Man and drink his blood, you don't have life in yourselves. He who eats my flesh and drinks my blood has eternal life, and I will raise him up at the last day. For my flesh is food indeed, and my blood is drink indeed. He who eats my flesh and drinks my blood lives in me, and I in him—'"

"That's Communion!" I blurted.

Shep continued reading. "'As the living Father sent me, and I live because of the Father; so he who feeds on me, he will also live because of me. This is the bread which came down out of heaven—not as our fathers ate the manna, and died. He who eats this bread will live forever.' He said these things in the synagogue, as he taught in Capernaum. Therefore many of his disciples, when they heard this, said, 'This is a hard saying! Who can listen to it?'"

I interjected myself again. "Wow! Nothing changes, does it. They found Jesus' words hard to take back then, just like people do today."

"That's right. But we're not done yet. Keep listening." Shep began to read, "But Jesus knowing in himself that his disciples murmured at this, said to them, 'Does this cause you to stumble? Then what if you would see the Son of Man ascending to where he was before? It is the spirit who gives life. The flesh profits nothing. The words that I speak to you are spirit, and are life. But there are some of you who don't believe.'" Shep slid past a line of words and said, "At this, many of his disciples went back, and walked no more with him. Jesus said therefore to the twelve, 'You don't also want to go away, do you?' Simon Peter answered him, 'Lord, to whom would we go? You have the words of eternal life. We have come to believe and know that you are the Christ, the Son of the living God.'"

Shep closed his New Testament and slid it to the side.

Amazed, I said, "We actually have a Bible passage that shows disciples turning away from Jesus because He said we have to eat the bread that is His body to have life eternal?"

"It's a hard teaching, but like Peter said, Jesus is the one with the words of eternal life. If He says the bread is His body, it is His body. We trust Him, because 'we have come to believe and know' that He is our Messiah, the Son of the living God."

Shep looked out at the cold winter night and then tipped his head back, directing his face toward the lightbulb above the booth, as if to bask in what little heat it gave off.

Out of the corner of my eye I saw the waitress by the café's entrance. She flipped over the 'open' and 'closed' sign. "I guess it's about that time," I said.

Shep sighed, "I guess so." He plucked his beanie from the mound of clothing next to him. "I have really appreciated our conversation," he said.

"Me, too," I said, "Thank you for answering my questions."

"It was my pleasure."

"Shep," I said, "Do you have a place to go?"

He looked at me and flashed a warm half-smile. "Of course I do. I've come to believe in Him who has the word of life."

I wanted to push for more, but I didn't. Maybe I should have, but I didn't. Instead I thanked him again for inviting me to his booth and for being my shepherd. His restrained laugh emerged, and he said, "It's been my privilege to serve you in the Word. I pray you understand the faithfulness of closed Communion now."

"Much better than before," I said.

"Praise be to God," Shep said, "Maybe you'll be willing to go back to the closed Communion church?"

"I think I will," I said.

"Ask questions," Shep said, "The pastor will be happy to provide answers and guidance as best he can. That's why he's there, to be a shepherd, to show you Jesus in Word and Sacrament."

I pulled out some money and left it on the table. Shep started to do the same but I stopped him. "Please, paying for your coffee is the least

I can do." He put up some resistance, but I insisted.

"Well, thank you," he said as he pulled his beanie onto his head.

We both gathered our coats and pushed our arms into them as we stood up. We made small talk on the way to the café door, but to be honest I got lost in my thoughts when I saw the sign the waitress had flipped over. It was a typical reversible open and closed sign. The side facing me read, "come in, we are open." As Shep and I went through the door and into the snowy wind, I looked back at the sign, which said, "sorry, we are closed."

I thought about Shep's café analogy and how it was a good thing the Church wasn't exactly like a café. If churches had signs on their doors like cafés do, they would read slightly different. When it came to Communion, the heterodox churches would display a sign that read, "sorry, we are open." If, on the other hand, an orthodox church was to hang up a sign, it would say, "come in, we are closed."

Acknowledgments

THANK you, Jessica, for assisting me in the writing process. More than that, thank you for introducing me to orthodox Christianity.

Rev. Holthus, thank you for providing solid Biblical answers to my questions, especially regarding the Lord's Supper. You were my first Shep and because of you I learned of the Lord's love in closed Communion.

Thank you Ray and Beth for editing this work. Gaven, your foreword is greatly appreciated. Thank you for putting pen to paper in service to those who read this book.

Dear reader, thank you for engaging Shep in this conversation on closed Communion. I pray that you have been blessed by what you read. My hope is that this thin volume helped you see the Lord's love in His Sacramental meal.

About the Author

TYREL Bramwell lives with his wife and children in Ferndale, California where he is the pastor of St. Mark's Evangelical Lutheran Church (Lutheran Church - Missouri Synod). His writing aims to enrich readers with a worldview that is packed with imagination, yet rooted in the knowable and absolute truth of the Triune God's Word. He has a bachelor's degree from Concordia University–Ann Arbor, Michigan and his master of divinity degree from Concordia Theological Seminary in Fort Wayne, Indiana.

He is online at tyrelbramwell.com

Other books by Tyrel Bramwell

The Gift and the Defender (Lumen Legends, Book One)

Finding the Truth in Story: Grimm's Fairy Tales, Vol. I

The World of the Wazzlewoods: A Fern & Dale Fairy Tale

Order yours today!

tyrelbramwell.com | amazon.com

If you enjoyed this book, please give it a review online. Positive reviews help tremendously.

Made in the USA
Lexington, KY
03 November 2018